NACUBO's Guide to Unitizing Investment Pools
Second Edition

Mary S. Wheeler

NACUBO

Library of Congress Cataloging-in-Publication Data

Wheeler, Mary S.
  NACUBO's guide to unitizing investment pools / by Mary S. Wheeler. -- 2nd ed.
     p. cm.
  Includes bibliographical references and index.
  ISBN 978-0-915164-23-3 (alk. paper)
 1. Endowments--United States--Handbooks, manuals, etc. 2. Education--United States--Finance--Handbooks, manuals, etc. I. National Association of College and University Business Officers. II. Title.

 LB2336.W47 2011
 378.1'06--dc22

                                        2011004093

Author: Mary S. Wheeler
Design and Production Management: Kaysha Johnston, NACUBO

National Association of College and University Business Officers
Washington, DC
www.nacubo.org

Printed in the United States of America

contents

ACKNOWLEDGEMENTS

Since the National Association of College and University Business Officers' (NACUBO) first edition was published in 1993, the operational complexities surrounding endowment management have not let up. Ever challenging economic pressure and changes in laws that address endowments have led to increasingly varied investment vehicles. Although investment pools enable extensive asset diversification, the need to monitor the activity and balances of donor restricted endowment funds necessitates a thorough understanding of fund tracking methods, of which unitization is the most common approach. Although unitization is not new to higher education, the time had come to modernize the concepts and practices from the 1993 publication.

NACUBO acknowledges the following individuals for their support and guidance in the development of *NACUBO's Guide to Unitizing Investment Pools, Second Edition*.

We are grateful to **Mary S. Wheeler,** Assistant Vice President for Finance, Stevens Institute of Technology, who wrote the guide and **Karen Craig**, NACUBO Technical Advisor, who managed the effort.

The edition was influenced by a dedicated group of business officers, most particularly **Dale C. Larson**, Vice President Business & Finance Dallas Theological Seminary; **Jason A. Little**, Assistant Controller, Accounting & Financial Services and **Jason Schroeder**, Senior Manager both from University of Notre Dame; **Debra J. Martin**, Vice President and Associate Dean for Finance and Administration, Loyola Marymount University, Loyola Law School; **Karl E. Turro**, Controller Northwestern University; **Carolee E. White**, Assistant Treasurer and Director, Investments, Colgate University; and **Susan Budak**, author of NACUBO's Financial Accounting and Reporting Manual and AICPA Not-for-Profit Industry Expert Panel Leader.

For her dedication, leadership, and constructive critique we also thank NACUBO's Director of Accounting Policy, **Sue Menditto**.

SECTION I

INTRODUCTION

The concept of an endowment is relatively easy to understand. Like a personal savings account, money is set aside and the investment returns are compounded and withdrawn when needed. However, unlike a personal savings account or retirement account, donor-restricted endowments are expected to last forever. This requirement of lasting "in perpetuity" introduces the issue of retaining the purchasing power by protecting against inflation and maintaining intergenerational equity—so that current and future beneficiaries receive equivalent value from the endowment.

Adding to the complexity, donors generally establish endowments to provide funds for specific purposes, and institutions may have thousands of named funds to manage, all with specific donor instructions.

Questions arising from these overarching considerations include the following:

1. What is the right investment mix to generate sufficient investment returns for current use while protecting purchasing power for the future?
2. What portion of investment returns should be used in the current period and what portion should be reinvested to grow the endowment?
3. What expenses are appropriate to charge to endowments?
4. Can spending continue when no accumulated investment returns are available—in other words, is it OK to borrow from the original principal on a temporary basis?
5. Should there be a minimum level at which an endowment fund is created? If yes, what is it and does it vary by purpose?

The answers may vary, as approaches will conform to the circumstances unique to each institution. Many guides, advisories, state laws, surveys, and consultants are available to help answer the questions noted above. In addition, suggested resources for addressing these issues are listed in Appendix C.

Drilling down further leads to some of the concepts and issues described in this guide—i.e., the practice of combining endowment assets into a consolidated investment pool, tracking the value of each individual fund, allocating investment returns, assessing fees, and meeting fiduciary and financial reporting requirements. This guide will:

- explain how to manage endowment funds within a consolidated investment pool,
- describe the basics of unitization,
- identify the pros and cons of unitization,
- explain the regulatory and reporting requirements that must be supported by a unitization method, and
- illustrate four methods of administering consolidated investment pools.

ENDOWMENTS

"The three principal categories of endowment and similar funds are true endowments, term endowments, and funds functioning as endowment (sometimes referred to as quasi-endowment funds or board-designated funds). True endowments are funds received from a donor with the restriction that the principal not be spent. Term endowments are funds for which the donor stipulates that the principal may be expended after a stated period of time or upon the occurrence of a certain event. Funds functioning as endowment are funds established by an institution's governing board that function like an endowment fund but may be expended at any time at the discretion of the board."[1] The authority to establish funds functioning as endowments may be delegated to management by the governing board. In addition, funds functioning as endowments or quasi-endowments may be established with restricted gifts from donors who request that their gifts be invested, with both the principal and the investment returns available for use at the discretion of the institution.

CONSOLIDATED INVESTMENT POOLS

Consolidated investment pools are the means by which organizations combine the assets of many endowments and other funds into one investment portfolio. Generally, the investment decisions for the pool are guided by high-level investment objectives that are achieved by specific asset allocations and ongoing due diligence procedures.

Pooling individual funds for investment purposes has many benefits, including but not limited to:

- spreading the total risk for each fund and making the risk equal for all pooled funds,
- enhancing the performance relative to that of a smaller fund,
- potentially reducing management fees,
- minimizing un-invested cash, and
- simplifying the accounting burden.[2]

After endowment assets are consolidated within an investment pool, it is not possible to attribute specific investment assets to specific endowment funds. Instead, each endowment fund "owns" an "interest" in the pool. "Unitizing" the pool is a method of tracking the ownership interests of each endowment fund. However, as demonstrated in Example 1, unitization is not required for tracking the endowment funds within a consolidated investment pool.

Although many institutions include pledges in their endowments, consolidated investment pools should not include pledges receivable, as the institution has not yet received any funds to invest. Therefore, when tracking the net assets of endowment and similar funds, care must be taken to segregate the portion of an endowment fund's assets represented by an interest in the investment pool from the portion of the assets that are represented by an outstanding pledge. Only the assets in the consolidated investment pool should be considered when allocating investment return, applying spending formulas, or assessing fees.

[1] NACUBO, "Endowment Management," in College and University Business Administration, Fifth Edition (Washington, DC: NACUBO, 1992), 7–8.
[2] Cambridge Associates LLC, Unitization: An Introduction (Boston, MA: Cambridge Associates LLC, 2003), 2.

THE REGULATORY AND REPORTING ENVIRONMENT

UMIFA and UPMIFA

Laws for managing charitable endowment funds are established at the state level and generally follow one of two uniform commercial code standards: the Uniform Management of Institutional Funds Act (UMIFA) or the Uniform Prudent Management of Institutional Funds Act (UPMIFA). UMIFA, promulgated in the 1970s, paved the way for a broader definition of "income" on endowment funds. UMIFA was a pioneering statute, providing uniform and fundamental rules for the investment of funds held by charitable institutions and the expenditure of funds donated as "endowments" to those institutions. Those rules supported two general principles: (1) that assets would be invested prudently in diversified investments that sought growth as well as income and (2) that appreciation of assets could prudently be spent for the purposes of any endowment fund held by a charitable institution.[3] UMIFA not only freed charity managers to delegate investment decisions to outside managers, but also allowed them to invest assets for long-term growth, not just current yields. The law also gave managers the freedom to invest in accordance with strategies that balanced risk and return by allocating investment assets among various classes, usually with a tilt toward stocks. The new law also made it possible to aggregate endowment assets into consolidated investment pools. All of this was revolutionary at the time.[4]

UPMIFA was promulgated in 2006 and provided more flexibility for organizations to manage their endowment funds. Viewing funds in a more holistic manner, UPMIFA eliminated a requirement contained in UMIFA whereby an organization may not spend below the historic dollar value of a fund. As of June 4, 2010, 48 states had adopted or introduced legislation modeled after UPMIFA.[5]

Under both UPMIFA and UMIFA, spending decisions about endowments must be considered at the individual fund level—not at the consolidated investment pool level. Therefore, although the assets of endowments may be combined for investment purposes, in order to support the organization's fiduciary responsibilities its systems must be able to track endowments at the individual fund level.

Financial Statement Presentation

Independent Institutions

Accounting and reporting guidance for endowment funds held by independent institutions is promulgated by the Financial Accounting Standards Board (FASB) and is contained in the Accounting Standards Codification (ASC) 958-205-05 and 958-205-45. [Refer to Appendix B for a crosswalk from the FASB ASC to the Statements of Financial Accounting Standards (SFAS) related to endowments and investments.]

A not-for-profit organization (NFP) shall report the net assets of an endowment fund in a statement of financial position within the three classes of net assets—permanently restricted, temporarily restricted, or unrestricted—based on the existence or absence of donor-imposed restrictions.[6]

The following is a description of the three classifications of net assets:

> Permanently restricted net assets arise from donor-imposed restrictions which stipulate that the resources be maintained permanently. However, the institution generally may expend all or part of the income or consume other economic benefits derived from the donated assets.

> Temporarily restricted net assets result from donor-imposed restrictions that permit the institution to expend the donated assets as specified and are satisfied by either the passage

---

[3] http://uniformlaws.org/ActSummary.aspx?title=Prudent Management of Institutional Funds Act

[4] Janne G. Gallagher, "Legal Brief: Been Down So Long, It Looks Like UMIFA to Me," *Foundation News & Commentary* 44, no. 2 (March/April 2003), http://www.foundationnews.org/CME/article.cfm?ID=2411.

[5] http://uniformlaws.org/ActSummary.aspx?title=Prudent Management of Institutional Funds Act

[6] FASB ASC 958-205-45-15

of time or actions of the institution. Temporarily restricted net assets may be restricted to support a particular operating activity, invested for a term (i.e., term endowment or split-interest agreement), used in a future period, or to acquire, renovate or maintain long-lived assets.

Unrestricted net assets include revenues for providing services for a fee (exchange transactions); unrestricted contributions; and realized and unrealized gains, dividends, and interest on investments which are neither permanently nor temporarily restricted.[7]

NFPs are required to carry their assets held for investment at fair value. ASC 958-305-45 paragraphs 22 through 24 contains rules for accounting for and disclosing "underwater" conditions, i.e., when the fair value of a donor-restricted endowment fund falls below the amount that is to be retained permanently. The portion of the endowment that is underwater is recorded as a reduction to unrestricted net assets.

With the widespread adoption of UPMIFA and the elimination of historic dollar value as a "floor" for spending, the FASB issued FSP FAS 117-1 (ASC 958-205) to provide guidance for institutions that are managing funds under UPMIFA, as well as to stipulate additional financial statement disclosures for all endowment funds, regardless of state law. Table 1 shows the endowment components and the net asset classifications for organizations in states operating under UPMIFA. As of this printing, forty six states and the District of Columbia have enacted UPMIFA and two states have introduced the law.

Table 1: Restriction Classifications of Endowments for Independent Institutions in States Following UPMIFA

Component	Net Asset Classification	
	Donor-Restricted Endowments	Board-Designated Endowments
Original gift or investment	Dependent on the organization's interpretation of the law as to the portion that must be retained permanently. The portion that is retained permanently is permanently restricted. The portion that is not required to be retained permanently is classified as temporarily restricted.	Unrestricted
Additional gift or investment		Unrestricted
Donor-directed or investor-directed reinvestment of return		Unrestricted
Accumulated investment return available for appropriation, i.e., • interest and dividends, • realized gains, and • unrealized gains.	Temporarily restricted until appropriated for spending	Unrestricted
Spending on endowments below the amount that must be retained permanently	Unrestricted	Not applicable
Negative investment return	Unrestricted	Unrestricted

[7] NACUBO *Financial Accounting and Reporting Manual (FARM)* 503.12

In addition to descriptions of the amount to be retained permanently and the organization's investment and spending policies, FASB also requires tabular disclosures for all organizations regardless of whether they are operating under UPMIFA, UMIFA, or other laws. The additional tabular disclosures that require details from an institution's financial system include:

- "the composition of the NFP's endowment by net asset class at the end of the period, in total and by type of endowment fund, showing donor-restricted endowment funds separately from board-designated endowment funds; and,
- a reconciliation of the beginning and ending balance of the NFP's endowment, in total and by net asset class, including, at a minimum, all of the following line items (that apply): investment return, separated into investment income (for example, interest, dividends, rents) and net appreciation or depreciation of investments; contributions; amounts appropriated for expenditure; reclassifications; and other changes."[8]

These disclosures are illustrated in tables 28, 29, 30, and 31 and in Tab 10 of the example spreadsheet.

To accommodate these reporting requirements, systems supporting the accounting and reporting of endowment funds for independent institutions must:

- track the portion of an endowment that must be retained permanently,
- quantify the investment return available for appropriation from each fund,
- account for the change in each endowment's value from the beginning to the end of the period attributable to the types of activity required for disclosure (i.e., contributions, investment returns, spending distributions, etc.) in sufficient detail to facilitate FASB and Internal Revenue Service reporting requirements,
- identify donor-restricted endowments for which the market value has dropped below the amount to be retained permanently, and
- aggregate the total of an organization's endowments by net asset category.

Public Institutions

Accounting and reporting guidance for endowment funds held by public institutions is promulgated by the Governmental Accounting Standards Board (GASB) and is contained in the following Statements of Government Accounting Standards (SGAS):

- Statement No. 34, Basic Financial Statements—and Management's Discussion and Analysis—for State and Local Governments (SGAS 34)
- Statement No. 35, Basic Financial Statements—and Management's Discussion and Analysis—for Public Colleges and Universities (SGAS 35)
- Statement No. 37, Basic Financial Statements—and Management's Discussion and Analysis—for State and Local Governments: Omnibus (SGAS 37)

The standards as they relate to endowment funds focus primarily on the classification of net assets, described as "the difference between assets and liabilities (i.e., the residual equity) of public institutions. GASB requires that public institutions display net assets in three components: invested in capital assets, net of related debt; restricted; and unrestricted. (When restricted expendable net assets are present, restricted net assets should be differentiated between restricted expendable and restricted nonexpendable net assets.)"[9]

[8] FASB ASC 958-205-50-1B(d) and (e)
[9] NACUBO *FARM* 350.1

Restricted net assets are defined in SGAS 34 as follows:

> Restricted net assets is the portion of net assets subject to externally-imposed constraints placed on their use by creditors (such as through debt covenants), grantors, contributors, or laws and regulations of other governments. When permanent endowments or permanent fund principal amounts are included, restricted net assets should be displayed in the statement of net assets in two additional components—expendable and nonexpendable. Nonexpendable net assets are those required to be retained in perpetuity.[10]

Based on these definitions, Table 2 contains the components of endowment funds and the net asset classifications under SGAS 34. These classifications are the same for endowments managed following either UMIFA or UPMIFA.

Table 2: Net Asset Classifications for Endowments Held by Public Institutions

Component	Net Asset Classification	
	Donor-Restricted Endowments	**Board-Designated Endowments**
Original gift	Restricted nonexpendable	
Additional gift	Restricted nonexpendable	
Donor-directed or investor-directed reinvestment of return	Restricted nonexpendable	
Investment of nongift source		Unrestricted
Investment of unrestricted expendable gift		Unrestricted
Investment of restricted expendable gift		Restricted expendable
Accumulated investment return available for appropriation, i.e., • interest and dividends, • realized gains, and • unrealized gains	Restricted expendable until appropriated for spending	Unrestricted
Spending on endowments below the amount that must be retained permanently	Per GASB Comprehensive Implementation Guide (CIG), question and answer 7.24.14, restricted nonexpendable net assets can be reduced to reflect the remaining value of the donor restricted endowment. GASB addressed the reduction of restricted nonexpendable net assets when UMIFA was in effect and has not provided additional guidance in response to UPMIFA.	Not applicable
Negative investment return	Per GASB Comprehensive Implementation Guide (CIG), question and answer 7.24.14, restricted nonexpendable net assets can be reduced to reflect the remaining value of the donor restricted endowment. GASB addressed the reduction of restricted nonexpendable net assets when UMIFA was in effect and has not provided additional guidance in response to UPMIFA.	Unrestricted

[10] SGAS 34, paragraphs 34 and 35

Although the endowment reporting for public institutions is less detailed than for independent institutions, being able to identify an endowment's component parts is important in meeting the organization's fiduciary responsibilities of managing donor-restricted endowments.

IRS Reporting

For independent institutions required to file IRS Form 990, Return of Organization Exempt From Income Tax, Schedule D Part V requires a roll forward of the endowment balance from the beginning of the year to the end of the year, showing contributions; net investment earnings, gains, and losses; grants or scholarships; other expenditures for facilities and programs; and administrative expenses. Also included in Schedule D Part V are the types of endowments making up the year-end balances, specifically the percentage of board-designated or quasi-endowments, permanent (true) endowments, and term endowments. Definitions of these terms are provided in the IRS instructions accompanying the form.

NACUBO-Commonfund Study of Endowments and Other Surveys

In addition to the financial statement reporting requirements, an organization may also wish to participate in the annual NACUBO-Commonfund Study of Endowments, which compiles information on endowments and investment pools across higher education. The study focuses on two levels: an organization's total endowment and its primary investment pool. Information gathered at the pool level includes asset allocations, spending policies, and investment performance. To the extent that an organization wishes to participate in this or similar studies and surveys conducted by other organizations, the reporting requirements of those institutional studies should also be considered.

Section II

Basics of Unitization

What Is Unitization?

A unitized accounting system is one that accounts for a fund's interest in an investment pool on the basis of units or shares. Like a mutual fund, each individual fund in an investment pool holds shares or units representing its proportionate share of the pool's investments. A unitized system establishes a procedure for determining the number of units a fund receives when it deposits money into the pool and the units redeemed when a specific dollar amount is withdrawn.[11] Unit transactions are based on the effective unit value at the time the transaction occurs.

Alternatives to Unitization

The alternative to unitization is to track endowment funds at their full dollar value within the accounting system. The investment pool's monthly investment returns are allocated and recorded to each fund based on its account balance and its proportionate share of the total pool. Application of spending rates and assessment of fees are also calculated and recorded at the fund level. This alternative is sometimes referred to as the "dollarized" method.

[11] SGAS 34, paragraphs 34 and 35

Pros and Cons of Unitization

Advantages and disadvantages of the unitized method and the dollarized method are shown in Table 3.

Table 3: Comparison of Investment Accounting Methods

Unitized Method	Dollarized Method
Advantages: • Unitization facilitates estimating the performance of the investment pool based on the change in unit value for the period. • It accommodates the use of a consolidated accumulation account from which spending and fees can be withdrawn rather than from each endowment fund. • Investment results can be posted at the pool level, rather than within each fund, which results in fewer transaction lines posted to the general ledger each month. • Unitization assists with identification of the principal portion of the fund, making it easier to assign the correct net asset restriction classifications to the account.	**Advantages:** • The dollar value of the fund within the general ledger represents the current market value of the fund. • Dollarization accommodates different payout percentages and fee arrangements by fund. • It requires posting only in dollars, rather than in both units and dollars.
Disadvantages: • Tracking the number of units for each fund requires a system capable of recording each principal transaction (new gift, withdrawal, reinvested payout) in units as well as dollars. • Assessing fees against a central accumulation account rather than recording them to each fund may be viewed as being less than transparent with donors or holders of quasi-endowments. • Accommodating different payout percentages or fee agreements by fund requires additional steps to adjust for the differences. • Determining the current market value of a fund requires multiplication of the number of units by the current market value per unit unless all distributed investment earnings are periodically recorded to each fund in the general ledger.	Disadvantages • Dollarization results in many lines of transactions posted to the general ledger each month, with each type of investment transaction allocated to each fund. • It requires that any change in value of the investment pool be allocated to each fund. • It requires separate accumulators to differentiate between the principal invested and the investment return, to quantify the net asset restriction classification within each fund.

Important issues to consider when choosing which method to use include the following:

1. The availability of systems to track both dollars and units
2. The number of funds within the pool with exceptions either to the spending policy or to the sharing of expenses / assessment of fees
3. The variables needed for calculating and applying the spending policy
4. The ease with which reporting systems can present periodic transaction reports and market values to end users

Section III

Administrative Decisions for Establishing a Unitized Pool

This section focuses on the administrative decisions that are required for establishing a unitized pool. These are in addition to the higher-level policy decisions regarding appropriate asset allocations, establishing the portion of donor-restricted endowment funds that are to be retained permanently, and developing a prudent spending policy. Those policy decisions are outside the scope of this guide and will vary from one institution to another.

The key administrative decisions include the following:

1. How often a unit value will be calculated
2. The unit value that will be used for unit transactions—the value at the beginning of the period or the value at the end of the period
3. Which transactions will purchase units and which transactions will increase the unit value
4. How the unit "book value" used for calculating the gain or loss on withdrawals from the unitized pool will be tracked—"first in, first out" (FIFO); "last in, first out" (LIFO); or average cost

The outcome of these decisions will allow an institution to establish procedures for recording endowment fund transactions so that the proportionality of each individual fund to the whole pool is calculated consistently from period to period. It is important to establish and apply consistent practices across all endowment funds participating in the investment pool in order to meet fiduciary responsibilities and foster strong donor relations and stewardship.

How Often Will a Unit Value Be Calculated?

Most unitized pools are administered using a monthly or quarterly unit value. Factors to consider when making the choice include how frequently cash is moved to and from the investment pool, how often endowment gifts are posted to the general ledger, and how often the organization wishes to report on the market value of the pool. If these are all on a monthly basis, then a monthly unit value will result in more accurate allocations and measurements for each fund. If these tasks occur less frequently than monthly, then a quarterly unit value will likely suffice. An annual unit value is also a possibility but will result in the least amount of precision for managing endowment funds.

What Unit Value Will Be Used for Unit Transactions—the Value at the Beginning of the Period or the Value at the End of the Period?

Once the frequency of the unit value calculation is decided, the second question is whether to base the unit transactions on the value at the beginning of the period or the end of the period. Factors to consider when deciding are listed in Table 4.

Table 4: Determining the Unit Value for Unit Transactions

Unit Value at the Beginning of the Period	Unit Value at the End of the Period
Considerations:	Considerations:
• Investments in the pool for a portion of the period will receive investment returns as if the money had been invested for the entire period. • Unit transactions for gifts and quasi- endowment investments are processed as received during the period as soon as the unit value is calculated based on the investment market value at the end of the previous period. For example, a gift received on September 15 will purchase units based on the market value per unit calculated as of August 31.	• Pool investment returns during the period are allocated only to those funds that were invested in the pool for the entire period. • Unit transactions are held for processing until after the unit value is calculated at the end of the period. For example, a gift received on September 15 will purchase units based on the market value per unit calculated as of September 30. • Investment income on gifts received during the period may generate unrestricted revenue to the organization.

One factor to consider when making this decision is how soon after the end of the period the market value of the investments is available to calculate the unit value. If it is more than a few days after the end of the month, then the organization may want to use the unit value from the beginning of the period, so as not to delay posting gifts to the endowment system or to require a two-step process (i.e., once to post the transactions in dollars and then a second step to calculate and post the transactions in units).

Another factor to consider is whether the endowment or accounting system can handle the more complicated "end of period" process. Example 4 illustrates transactions based on the unit value at the end of the period.

Whichever process is chosen, it is important to apply it consistently to both investments in and withdrawals from the consolidated pool.

Which Transactions Will Purchase Units and Which Transactions Will Increase the Unit Value?

One common approach to administering a unitized pool is to transact in units only when the transaction has an impact on the fund's principal (the Principal Only approach). Transactions that record the investment return or "spending" of the fund would have an effect on the unit value of the pool and be reflected in the fund's market value, but would not impact the number of units a fund holds. This approach results in significantly fewer transactions being recorded at the fund level but makes it more difficult to accommodate exceptions to the overall pool policies. This approach is illustrated in Example 2.

A second approach is to transact in units for all transactions that affect a fund's book value (the Book Value approach) and isolate the adjustment to market value represented by unrealized gains or losses to have an effect on the unit value only. This second approach makes it easier to handle exceptions to the spending policy or the application of fees, since a portion of the return and all the fees are recorded at the individual fund level. This approach is illustrated in Example 3.

Table 5 shows the transactions that may occur in an endowment fund invested in a consolidated investment pool using the Principal Only approach. Some of the transactions affect the principal of the fund and others are related to the investment return. Table 6 shows the endowment transactions based on the Book Value approach.

Table 5: Endowment Transactions, Principal Only Approach

Transaction Description	Affects Principal or Investment Return?	Transact in Units?
Gift received in an endowment fund / investment in a quasi-endowment fund	Principal	Yes
Allocation of investment pool return such as interest and dividends, realized gains and unrealized gains	Investment return	No
Application of spending policy and withdrawal of amounts available for spending	Investment return	No
Allocation of expenses or assessment of fees	Investment return	No
Reinvestment of unused amounts available for spending	Principal	Yes
Transfer from one fund to another within the pool	Principal	Yes
Withdrawal from a quasi-endowment	Principal	Yes
Divestment of an endowment fund from the pool to a separately held endowment	Principal	Yes

Table 6: Endowment Transactions, Book Value Approach

Transaction Description	Affects Principal or Investment Return?	Affects Book Value or Market Value?	Transact in Units?
Gift received in an endowment fund / investment in a quasi-endowment fund	Principal	Book value	Yes
Allocation of investment pool return: 1. Interest and dividends 2. Realized gains/losses 3. Unrealized gains/losses	Investment return	1. Book value 2. Book value 3. Market value	1. Yes 2. Yes 3. No
Application of spending policy and withdrawal of amounts available for spending	Investment return	Book value	Yes
Allocation of expenses or assessment of fees	Investment return	Book value	Yes
Reinvestment of unused amounts available for spending	Principal	Book value	Yes
Transfer from one fund to another within the pool	Principal	Book value	Yes
Withdrawal from a quasi-endowment	Principal	Book value	Yes
Divestment of an endowment fund from the pool to a separately held endowment	Principal	Book value	Yes

Factors to consider when choosing between the Principal Only approach and the Book Value approach are (1) how the spending policy is administered and (2) how investment returns are recorded in the investment pool. If the return is not recorded by interest/dividends, realized gains/losses, and unrealized gains/losses, then it will be difficult to transact in units for just a portion of the pool's overall investment return. Conversely, if application of the spending formula makes a distinction between interest/dividends (i.e., "yield") and the realized and unrealized gains or losses, it may be useful for interest and dividends to purchase units when they are allocated to each fund.

How Will the Unit "Book Value" Used for Calculating the Gain or Loss on Withdrawals From the Unitized Pool Be Tracked—"First In, First Out" (FIFO); "Last In, First Out" (LIFO); or Average Cost?

Regardless of the decisions described above, there are often situations in which a fund may redeem units from the investment pool. Common situations include withdrawals from quasi-endowments or divestments of donor-restricted endowments that must be invested separately from the pool. In these cases, it is important to calculate the gain or loss on the redemption of the fund's "units" from the pool in order to attribute the portion of the return to which the fund is entitled.

Applying either FIFO or LIFO requires tracking and storing the information for each unit transaction, so that redemptions can be associated with specific units purchased. This is a level of precision that is likely unnecessary and administratively burdensome. The more common practice is the use of average cost, in which only two variables are needed: the number of units held and the dollars recorded in the fund. The average cost per unit is the total dollars divided by the number of units. This amount is then compared with the unit value applied to the withdrawal to calculate the gain or loss on withdrawal. All three unitization model examples in this guide utilize the average cost method.

This question does not apply to investment pools managed using the dollarized method since all transactions and investment returns are recorded in each fund on a periodic basis. Therefore, withdrawals are based on the dollar amount only.

SECTION IV

EXAMPLES

The unitization methods illustrated in this guide meet the requirements of financial statement reporting for both independent and public institutions, as well as the information requested as part of the NACUBO-Commonfund Study of Endowments and IRS Form 990.

For purposes of comparing methods, the funds and transactions are the same throughout the examples, including the dollarized method. However, as noted below, the spending policy for the dollarized method is applied on a fund-by-fund basis, not on the entire pool. Therefore, the spending policy amount calculated in Example 1 (the dollarized method) differs from the amount calculated for the other three methods. As a result, the balance of the total pool under the dollarized method differs more than the balances calculated using the other methods.

To simplify the examples, calculations are performed quarterly rather than monthly. However, as previously noted, a monthly calculation is more equitable to donors and other investors in the pool. For illustrative purposes, only one quarter is shown for each example. The spreadsheet from which the tables are extracted can be found online (See Appendix C, University Sample Data). These spreadsheets display much more detail, include formulas, and can be downloaded for your use and experimentation.

Note: The examples are illustrated using an excel spreadsheet. Many institutions, however, use relational databases or third-party software programs to manage their consolidated investment pools. These other programs may be more efficient and may minimize reporting and control risk. Options include embedded functionality in general ledger programs, "fund accounting" services provided by custodian banks, or third-party software applications.

Sample Management Policies

Table 7 describes the policies that are consistent across all four examples.

Table 7: Policies Consistent for Dollarized and Unitized Calculation Methods

Spending policy	Spending is 4.0%, based on the average market value of the previous 12 quarters, measured after the second quarter of the current fiscal year for the upcoming fiscal year. For the dollarized method, if 12 quarters are not available, only the information for the number of quarters the fund has existed is averaged.
Payout	The payout amount is calculated and made available quarterly in accordance with the spending policy.
Fees	A 1.0% annual fee is assessed quarterly (0.25% per quarter), based on the market value at the end of the prior quarter.
Governing law	The state has passed legislation modeled on UPMIFA.
Donor-restricted funds to be retained permanently	The governing board has interpreted the law in its state to require that historic dollar value be retained permanently over the long term. Prudent spending, however, may allow funds to drop below historic dollar value on a temporary basis if not prohibited by the terms of the gift.

Endowment Funds Data

Table 8 shows the data for each of the eight example university endowment funds. It should be noted that some of the funds are donor-restricted endowments and others are board-designated. Some of the donor-restricted endowments are prohibited from spending when the fund's market value is below the historic dollar value ("underwater"), based on the terms of the gift agreement.

Donor instructions for Fund D require that the fund's investment returns be reinvested to principal until the fund reaches $250,000. As such, no funds are made available for spending, and all the investment returns are permanently restricted and accumulate until the fund reaches the threshold of $250,000, as per the terms of the agreement.

Table 8: Data for Example University Endowment Funds

Fund Name	A	B	C	D	E	F	G	H	Total All Funds
Type of Endowment	Donor-restricted	Board Designated	Donor-restricted	Donor-restricted	Board Designated	Board Designated	Donor-restricted	Donor-restricted	
Market Value at June 30 EOY 0	$210,000.00	$25,000.00	$165,000.00	$45,800.00	$73,000.00	$-	$-	$-	$518,800.00
Historic Gift Value at June 30 EOY 0	$185,000.00	N/A	$162,000.00	$40,000.00	N/A	N/A	N/A	$387,000.00	
Fee percentage	1.0%	1.0%	0.5%	0.0%	1.0%	1.0%	0.5%	1.0%	
Exceptions to fee policy	0.0%	0.0%	0.5%	1.0%	0.0%	0.0%	0.5%	0.00	
Payout while fund accumulates?	Yes	Yes	Yes	No	Yes	Yes	Yes	Yes	
Payout Underwater?	Yes	N/A	No	Yes	N/A	N/A	Yes	No	
12 Qtr Avg MV as of Dec 31 Year 0	$110,772.42	$15,714.29	$131,566.42	$22,740.00	$32,970.00	N/A	N/A		
12 Qtr Avg MV as of Dec 31 Year 1	$172,542.67	$18,202.09	$151,221.58	$32,871.25	$48,413.25				
12 Qtr Avg MV as of Dec 31 Year 2	$239,019.50	$19,462.00	$173,449.58	$53,965.33	$87,456.25	$36,183.00	$47,034.80	$628,801.40	
12 Qtr Avg MV as of Dec 31 Year 3	$302,458.79	$18,178.86	$208,903.14	$77,464.36	$118,718.29	$23,921.93	$60,456.21	$789,317.14	

Per the University's policy, fees are 1% unless otherwise noted.

Exceptions to the standard fee policy are typically the result of negotiations with a donor. Agreements should be read carefully to determine whether exceptions have been made.

The authority to payout on a fund that is underwater is based on donor instructions, management policies and relevant law.

To determine whether restrictions on payout exist, the donor agreement or management policies (depending on the type of endowment fund) should be consulted.

Three Years of Transaction Data

Table 9 shows the three years of transactions for each of the eight endowment funds. Positive amounts represent original gifts and/or additional gifts added to the fund. Negative amounts represent withdrawals from the fund.

Table 9: Transaction Data for Eight Endowment Funds

Fund Name		A	B	C	D	E	F	G	H	Total All Funds
Type of Endowment		Donor-restricted	Board Designated	Donor-restricted	Donor-restricted	Board Designated	Board Designated	Donor-restricted	Donor-restricted	
Year	Quarter									
1	1	50,000								50,000
1	2		(10,000)	20,000				25,000	500,000	535,000
1	3				30,000					30,000
1	4					100,000	35,000	25,000		160,000
2	1	50,000								50,000
2	2			20,000		(50,000)		25,000	500,000	495,000
2	3									-
2	4							25,000		25,000
3	1									-
3	2			20,000					500,000	520,000
3	3					(25,000)				(25,000)
3	4				30,000					30,000
Total Transactions		100,000	(10,000)	60,000	60,000	25,000	35,000	100,000	1,500,000	1,870,000
Additions to Principal		100,000	-	60,000	60,000	-	-	100,000	1,500,000	1,820,000

Three Years of Investment Returns Data

Table 10 shows the investment returns of the pool for the three years. These returns are used to calculate the payout amount in each of the examples. Returns are separately presented by type (i.e., interest/dividends, realized and unrealized gains/losses) to facilitate calculations in the various examples. This level of detail may or may not be applicable to all examples or all funds. The interval (i.e., monthly, quarterly, or annually) at which returns are calculated varies based on actual practice.

Table 10: Investment Returns Data for Eight Endowment Funds

Year	Month	Int/div	Compounding Factor	Quarterly Int/Div	Realized G/L	Compounding Factor	Quarterly Realized G/L	Unrealized G/L	Compounding Factor	Quarterly Unrealized G/L	Monthly Return	Quarterly Compound Return	Annual Compound Return	Quarterly Int/Div	Annual Int/Div Compounded	Quarterly Realized G/L	Annual Realized Gains Compounded
1	1	0.20%	100.20%		0.50%	100.50%		0.70%	100.70%		1.40%						
1	2	0.10%	100.10%		0.80%	100.80%		0.40%	100.40%		1.30%						
1	3	0.15%	100.15%	0.45%	-0.60%	99.40%	0.70%	1.15%	101.15%	2.27%	0.70%	3.44%		0.45%		0.70%	
1	4	0.06%	100.06%		0.75%	100.75%		-3.11%	96.89%		-2.30%						
1	5	0.30%	100.30%		0.80%	100.80%		-0.60%	99.40%		0.50%						
1	6	0.10%	100.10%	0.46%	0.30%	100.30%	1.86%	2.10%	102.10%	-1.67%	2.50%	0.64%		0.46%		1.86%	
1	7	0.05%	100.05%		0.00%	100.00%		2.25%	102.25%		2.30%						
1	8	0.40%	100.40%		2.00%	102.00%		-2.80%	97.20%		-0.40%						
1	9	0.03%	100.03%	0.48%	0.50%	100.50%	2.51%	1.17%	101.17%	0.55%	1.70%	3.62%		0.48%		2.51%	
1	10	0.40%	100.40%		1.40%	101.40%		0.75%	100.75%		2.30%						
1	11	0.15%	100.15%		0.30%	100.30%		1.40%	101.40%								
1	12	0.90%	100.90%	1.37%	-0.60%	99.40%	0.88%	-0.82%	99.18%	-0.50%	-0.52%	1.76%	9.77%	1.37%	2.79%	0.88%	6.07%
2	1	0.32%	100.32%		0.09%	100.09%		-0.42%	99.58%		-0.01%						
2	2	0.60%	100.60%		0.00%	100.00%		0.15%	100.15%		0.80%						
2	3	0.07%	100.07%	0.87%	3.00%	103.00%	3.15%	-1.37%	98.63%	-0.83%	1.70%	3.23%		0.87%		3.15%	
2	4	0.20%	100.20%		0.10%	100.10%		0.40%	100.40%		0.70%						
2	5	0.08%	100.08%		0.80%	100.80%		1.32%	101.32%		1.35%						
2	6	0.05%	100.05%	0.53%	0.65%	100.65%	1.79%	1.07%	101.07%	3.70%	1.00%	4.31%		0.53%		1.79%	
2	7	0.03%	100.03%		0.80%	100.80%		-0.95%	99.05%		1.40%						
2	8	0.42%	100.42%		0.06%	100.06%		0.67%	100.67%		0.90%						
2	9	0.60%	100.60%	0.68%	0.00%	100.00%	0.06%	0.40%	100.40%	0.11%	1.50%	2.62%		0.68%		0.06%	
2	10	0.80%	100.80%		1.90%	101.90%		1.27%	101.27%		0.10%						
2	11	0.09%	100.09%		0.00%	100.00%		0.16%	100.16%		-0.60%						
2	12	0.60%	100.60%	1.50%	0.06%	100.06%	0.65%	0.67%	100.67%	0.06%	-0.10%	2.21%	12.94%	1.50%	3.63%	0.65%	5.74%
3	1	0.08%	100.08%		0.00%	100.00%		0.70%	100.70%		0.00%						
3	2	0.30%	100.30%		0.90%	100.90%		-4.52%	95.48%		-3.15%						
3	3	0.08%	100.08%	0.43%	-0.70%	99.30%	0.73%	-0.08%	99.92%	-0.09%	-2.60%	1.09%		0.43%		0.73%	
3	4	0.50%	100.50%		0.00%	100.00%		-2.00%	98.00%		1.10%						
3	5	0.10%	100.10%		3.00%	103.00%		1.05%	101.05%		1.90%						
3	6	0.05%	100.05%	0.68%	0.80%	100.80%	3.00%	0.32%	100.32%	-5.11%	-0.20%	-1.53%		0.68%		3.00%	
3	7	0.08%	100.08%		0.00%	100.00%		-1.44%	98.56%		-3.15%						
3	8	0.47%	100.47%		0.90%	100.90%		-0.70%	99.30%		0.00%						
3	9	0.20%	100.20%	0.76%	0.00%	100.00%	0.19%	0.60%	100.60%	-5.38%	0.20%	-4.41%		0.76%		0.19%	
3	10	0.09%	100.09%		0.60%	100.60%		0.74%	100.74%		-1.50%						
3	11	0.30%	100.30%		2.00%	102.00%		-1.59%	98.41%		1.64%						
3	12	0.70%	100.70%	1.09%	0.00%	100.00%	2.61%	-2.80%	97.20%	-2.85%	-2.10%	0.80%	-4.09%	1.09%	2.99%	2.61%	6.66%

Example 1—Dollarized Method

For this example, the following assumptions are used:

1. All investment returns and fees are allocated quarterly to each fund.
2. Allocations are based on balances at the beginning of the quarter.
3. The spending policy is applied on an individual fund basis. If 12 quarters are not available, the rate (4%) is applied to an average of the number of quarters in which the fund has existed. At the fund level, the amount of the spending policy payout for each year is fixed at the start of each year.
4. Note that Fund D is not receiving a payout while the fund accumulates. As a result, no payout is calculated or withdrawn from the fund. All the accumulated investment return is considered permanently restricted, as per the terms of the gift agreement.

Because the dollars recorded in each fund include both permanently restricted net assets and temporarily restricted net assets, some differentiation is required within the financial system to report the two different net asset classifications.

Tables 11, 12, and 13 illustrate the dollarized method of managing the investment pool.

Table 11 shows the activity at the pool level and at the fund level.

Table 11: Pool-Level and Fund-Level Activity for Example

Pool Level

	Market Value BOQ					Market Value EOQ
Total Pool	$2,421,112	0.80%	4.00%		$30,000	$2,452,754

Quarterly return from Table 10.

Fees are calculated at the fund level based on the information included in Table 8

Fund Level

Dollars	Market Value BOQ	Pro-Rata Share of Total	Allocate Performance	Total Fees	Assess Fees	Calculate Payout	Calculate Payout	Transactions	Market Value EOQ
Fund A	$329,539	13.62%	$2,638		$(824)	$(2,390)		$-	$328,963
Fund B	$15,660	0.65%	$126		$(39)	$(195)		$-	$15,552
Fund C	$236,612	9.77%	$1,892		$(296)	$(1,734)		$-	$236,474
Fund D	$86,840	3.59%	$695		$-	$-		$30,000	$117,535
Fund E	$109,291	4.51%	$874		$(273)	$(875)		$-	$109,017
Fund F	$35,911	1.48%	$287		$(90)	$(362)		$-	$35,746
Fund G	$101,783	4.20%	$813		$(127)	$(470)		$-	$101,999
Fund H	$1,505,476	62.18%	$12,044		$(3,764)	$(6,288)		$-	$1,507,468
Total	**$2,421,112**	**100.00%**	**$19,369**		**$(5,413)**	**$(12,314)**		**$30,000**	**$2,452,754**

At the pool level header row: Total Performance $19,369 | Total Fees $(5,413) | Calculate Payout $(12,314) | Transactions $30,000

Allocation of return is calculated based on pro-rata share of tthe pool

The principal balance information presented in Table 12 is necessary for calculating payout by fund. Note that until Year 0, each fund was invested separately.

Table 12: Principal Balance Information for Example 1

Period	Fund							
	A	B	C	D	E	F	G	H
Q1	50,000	-	110,000	-	15,000	-	-	-
Q2	50,865	-	113,000	-	15,600	-	-	-
Q3	51,004	-	114,000	10,000	20,400	-	-	-
Q4	43,000	-	110,000	8,800	19,900	-	-	-
Q5	101,000	-	135,000	8,700	19,700	-	-	-
Q6	103,000	10,000	137,000	19,000	29,700	-	-	-
Q7	113,000	11,000	140,000	19,800	30,000	-	-	-
Q8	112,600	10,800	138,797	30,000	29,800	-	-	-
Q9	162,800	10,900	140,000	31,500	32,000	-	-	-
Q10	175,000	20,900	140,000	31,600	42,000	-	-	-
Q11	180,000	22,900	145,000	33,000	43,100	-	-	-
Q12 (12/31 Year 0)	187,000	23,500	156,000	35,000	63,100	-	-	-
Q13	195,000	24,000	160,000	45,000	68,600	-	-	-
Q14 (6/30 Year 0)	210,000	25,000	165,000	45,800	73,000	-	-	-
Q15	265,592	25,640	169,153	47,376	74,998	-	-	-
Q16 (12/31 Year 1)	265,520	15,583	188,709	47,679	74,961	-	25,000	500,000
Q17	273,361	15,949	193,989	79,406	77,158	-	25,875	516,848
Q18 (6/30 Year 1)	276,384	16,033	195,844	80,803	177,992	35,000	51,299	524,652
Q19	332,893	16,329	200,412	83,413	182,814	36,044	52,893	540,285
Q20 (12/31 Year 2)	344,684	16,810	227,283	87,007	139,752	37,505	80,107	1,062,222
Q21 (12/31 Year 2)	351,136	17,025	231,447	89,286	142,579	38,394	82,103	1,087,394
Q22 (6/30 Year 2)	356,296	17,174	234,761	91,260	144,889	39,145	108,816	1,108,707
Q23	356,899	17,124	235,292	92,254	145,232	39,111	109,396	1,111,732
Q24 (12/31 Year 3)	348,156	16,625	249,663	90,842	141,773	38,051	107,116	1,585,656
Q25	329,539	15,660	236,612	86,840	109,291	35,911	101,783	1,505,476
Q26 (6/30 Year 3)	328,963	15,552	236,474	117,535	109,017	35,746	101,999	1,507,468

Table 13 shows the various calculations needed to test for underwater conditions and to track the accumulated appreciation.

Table 13: Historic Dollar Value, Underwater Test, and Accumulated Appreciation Calculations for Example 1

Historic Dollar Value	HDV BOQ	Transactions	HDV EOQ
Fund A	$285,000	-	$285,000
Fund B	N/A	N/A	N/A
Fund C	$222,000	-	$222,000
Fund D	$70,000	$30,000	$100,000
Fund E	N/A	N/A	N/A
Fund F	N/A	N/A	N/A
Fund G	$100,000	-	$100,000
Fund H	$1,500,000	-	$1,500,000
	$2,177,000	$30,000	$2,207,000

Underwater Test True = not UW False = UW"	BOQ Balances	EOQ Balances
Fund A	TRUE	TRUE
Fund B	N/A	N/A
Fund C	TRUE	TRUE
Fund D	TRUE	TRUE
Fund E	N/A	N/A
Fund F	N/A	N/A
Fund G	TRUE	TRUE
Fund H	TRUE	TRUE

> Donor-restricted funds are tested to determine if they are underwater for purposes of determining the appropriate payout amount. If the historic dollar value is less than the market value of the fund then it is deemed to be underwater.

> For donor-restricted funds, the EOQ HDV is subtracted from the EOQ market value to determine the accumulated appreciation.

Accumulated appreciation	EOQ Accumulated appreciation
Fund A	$43,963
Fund B	
Fund C	$14,474
Fund D	$17,535
Fund E	
Fund F	
Fund G	$1,999
Fund H	$7,468
	$85,439

Example 2—Unitized Method 1: Principal Only Approach, Transactions Based on Beginning-of-Quarter Values

Example 2 illustrates a unitized method of managing the investment pool. For this example, the following assumptions are used:

1. Only fund additions and fund withdrawals affect units. (Table 14 summarizes the effect on principal and transactions in units.)

Table 14: Effects on Principal or Investment Return and on Transaction in Units for Example 2

Transaction Description	Affects Principal or Investment Return	Transact in Units?
Gift received in an endowment fund / investment in a quasi-endowment fund	Principal	Yes
Allocation of investment pool return such as interest and dividends, realized gains and unrealized gains	Investment return	No
Application of spending policy and withdrawal of amounts available for spending	Investment return	No
Allocation of expenses or assessment of fees	Investment return	No
Reinvestment of unused amounts available for spending	Principal	Yes
Transfer from one fund to another within the pool	Principal	Yes
Withdrawal from a quasi-endowment	Principal	Yes
Divestment of an endowment fund from the pool to a separately held endowment	Principal	Yes

2. Transactions are based on unit values at the beginning of the quarter.

3. The unit value is calculated quarterly.

4. Withdrawals are based on average cost.

5. The spending policy is calculated and based on the pool's market value per unit and applied to each fund based on the number of units held at the start of each quarter. At the fund level, the spending policy payout per unit is set, but the annual amount may vary, depending on the units held by the fund each quarter.

6. Note that Fund D is not receiving a payout while the fund accumulates. To accomplish this in a unitized model, a payout is calculated and then added back to the fund in both dollars and by purchasing units. This amount increases the fund's principal. The accumulated undistributed investment returns are also considered permanently restricted, as per the terms of the gift agreement.

7. Exceptions to fees at the fund level are "adjusted" by adding units to the fund to negate the impact of the fees on the unit value. The formula compares the allowed fee to the stated fee policy to determine the percentage required to negate the effect of the fee assessed at the pool level. For example, Fund C is assessed a fee of only 0.5%, even though the fee policy is

1.0%. Therefore, the allowed fee is one-half (50%) of the fee policy. The formula to adjust for this exception to the fee policy is [Fund C fee base] * [fee policy rate (1.0%)] * 50%.

8. For underwater funds with parameters that prohibit a payout, the spending policy is not applied and no payout is calculated or withdrawn from the pool for that fund. Because the withdrawal of the payout affects the unit value per share for all funds, those funds that did not receive a payout are assigned additional shares to counteract the effect of the payout withdrawal. The formula to add units is

    a–Calculate the payout per unit: X
    b–Multiply the payout per unit by the number of units in funds without payout: Y
    c–Calculate the dollar value of the payout on the funds that did not receive payout: X * Y = Z
    d–Divide the dollar value (Z) by the market value per unit (MVU) to get the number of units to add to the funds that did not receive a payout: Z ÷ MVU = units to add

9. For the donor-restricted endowments, the dollar value recorded as "principal" in the financial system is the historic dollar value and is classified as permanently restricted net assets. The difference between the market value of the fund (units * market value per unit) and the actual dollars recorded in the fund is temporarily restricted, until appropriated for spending.

Tables 15 and 16 illustrate the unitized method of managing the investment pool. For illustrative purposes, only one quarter is shown. The spreadsheet from which the tables are extracted can be found online (See Appendix C, University Sample Data).

Table 15: Pool-Level Activity for Example 2

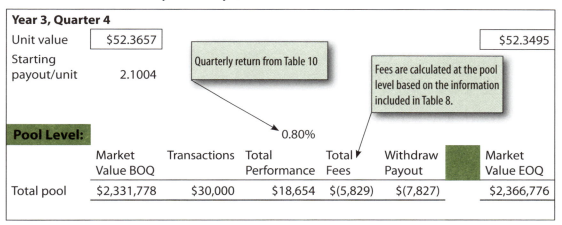

Year 3, Quarter 4							
Unit value	$52.3657						$52.3495
Starting payout/unit	2.1004						
				0.80%			
Pool Level:							
	Market Value BOQ	Transactions	Total Performance	Total Fees	Withdraw Payout		Market Value EOQ
Total pool	$2,331,778	$30,000	$18,654	$(5,829)	$(7,827)		$2,366,776

Quarterly return from Table 10

Fees are calculated at the pool level based on the information included in Table 8.

29

Table 16: Fund-Level Activity for Example 2

Year 3, Quarter 4

Unit Value	$52.3657
Starting payout/unit	2.1004

Fund Level

Dollars	Fund Principle BOQ	Market Value BOQ	Transactions	Gain/Loss on Withdrawal	Fee exception	Return Payout	Fund Principal EOQ	Market Value EOQ
Fund A	$285,000	$316,301	-	-	-	-	$285,000	$316,209
Fund B	$15,196	$15,505	-	-	-	-	$15,196	$15,500
Fund C	$222,000	$227,609	-	-	3	-	$222,000	$227,541
Fund D	$77,717	$84,275	$30,000	-	2	$845	$108,562	$115,086
Fund E	$101,492	$102,121	-	-	-	-	$101,492	$102,089
Fund F	$35,000	$34,688	-	-	-	-	$35,000	$34,677
Fund G	$100,000	$97,684	-	$1	-	-	$100,000	$97,655
Fund H	$1,500,000	$1,453,591	-	-	-	-	$1,500,000	$1,458,019
Total	$2,336,405	$2,331,774	$30,000		$6	$845	$2,367,250	$2,366,776

> Affects fund principal only.

> Amounts used to calculate the number of units required to add back to the fund to adjust for the fees taken at the pool level. Amounts do not affect principal.

> To reinvest income if directed by the donor. Increases the historic dollar value.

Units	Total Units	Unit Transactions	Fee Exceptions	Return Payout	Total Units
Fund A	6040.299	0.000	0.000	0.000	6040.299
Fund B	296.086	0.000	0.000	0.000	296.086
Fund C	4346.522	0.000	0.057	0.000	4346.579
Fund D	1609.348	572.894	0.038	16.138	2198.418
Fund E	1950.146	0.000	0.000	0.000	1950.146
Fund F	662.413	0.000	0.000	0.000	662.413
Fund G	1865.422	0.000	0.019	0.000	1865.441
Fund H	27758.453	0.000	0.000	93.176	27851.629
Total	44528.688	572.894	0.115	109.314	45211.011

Table 17 shows the various calculations needed to track the average cost per unit, the test for underwater conditions, and the accumulated appreciation for each fund.

Table 17: Average Cost per Unit, Underwater Test, and Accumulated Appreciation Calculations for Example 2

Average Cost per Unit	End of Quarter
Fund A	$47.183
Fund B	$51.323
Fund C	$51.075
Fund D	$49.382
Fund E	$52.043
Fund F	$52.837
Fund G	$53.607
Fund H	$53.857

> Calculated by dividing the EOQ fund principal balance by the total units at the end of the quarter.

Underwater Test True = not UW False = UW	EOQ Balances
Fund A	TRUE
Fund B	N/A
Fund C	TRUE
Fund D	TRUE
Fund E	N/A
Fund F	N/A
Fund G	FALSE
Fund H	FALSE

> Donor-restricted funds are tested to determine if they are underwater for purposes of determining the appropriate payout amount. If the market value of the fund is less than the fund principal at the end of the quarter, the fund is deemed to be underwater.

Accumulated Appreciation	EOQ Accumulated Appreciation
Fund A	$31,209
Fund B	
Fund C	$5,541
Fund D	$6,524
Fund E	
Fund F	
Fund G	$(2,345)
Fund H	$(41,981)
	$(1,052)

> For donor-restricted funds, the EOQ principal balance is subtracted from the EOQ market value to determine the accumulated appreciation.

Example 3—Unitized Method 2: Book Value Approach, Transactions Based on Beginning-of-Quarter Values

Example 3 illustrates a unitized method of managing the investment pool using the following assumptions:

1. Fund additions and withdrawals, interest and dividends, and realized gains affect units. Unrealized gains/losses do not affect units. (Table 18 below summarizes the affect on principal, book or market value, and transactions in units.)

Table 18: Effects on Principal or Investment Return, Book Value or Market Value, and Transaction in Units for Example 3

Transaction Description	Affects Principal or Investment Return?	Affects Book Value or Market Value?	Transact in Units?
Gift received in an endowment fund/ investment in a quasi-endowment fund	Principal	Book value	Yes
Allocation of investment pool return: 1. Interest and dividends 2. Realized gains/losses 3. Unrealized gains/losses	Investment return	1. Book value 2. Book value 3. Market value	1. Yes 2. Yes 3. No
Application of spending policy and withdrawal of amounts available for spending	Investment return	Book value	Yes
Allocation of expenses or assessment of fees	Investment return	Book value	Yes
Reinvestment of unused amounts available for spending	Principal	Book value	Yes
Transfer from one fund to another within the pool	Principal	Book value	Yes
Withdrawal from a quasi-endowment	Principal	Book value	Yes
Divestment of an endowment fund from the pool to a separately held endowment	Principal	Book value	Yes

2. Transactions are based on unit values at the beginning of the quarter.

3. The unit value is calculated quarterly.

4. Withdrawals are based on average cost.

5. The spending policy is calculated and based on the pool's market value per unit and applied to each fund based on the number of units held at the start of each quarter. At the fund level, the spending policy payout per unit is set, but the annual amount may vary, depending on the units held by the fund each quarter.

6. Note that Fund D is not receiving a payout while the fund accumulates. Therefore, no payout is calculated or withdrawn from the fund. All the accumulated investment return is considered permanently restricted, as per the terms of the gift agreement.

7. Exceptions to fees at the fund level are "adjusted" by adding units to the fund to negate the impact of the fees on the unit value. The formula compares the allowed fee to the stated fee policy, to determine the percentage required to negate the affect of the fee assessed at the pool level. For example, Fund C is assessed a fee of only 0.5%, even though the fee policy is 1.0%. Therefore, the allowed fee is one-half (50%) of the fee policy. The formula to adjust for this exception to the fee policy is [Fund C fee base] * [fee policy rate (1.0%)] * 50%.

8. For funds underwater with fund parameters that prohibit payout, no payout is withdrawn from the investment return portion of the fund.

9. For the donor-restricted endowments, the dollar value recorded in the financial system as "principal" is the historic dollar value and is classified as permanently restricted net assets. The amount recorded as investment return represents accumulated unspent returns and is classified as temporarily restricted, until appropriated for spending. The difference between the total dollars recorded for principal and investment return, and the market value per unit times the number of units held by each fund, is the accumulated unrealized gain or loss on each fund. This amount is temporarily restricted, until appropriated for spending.

Table 19 shows the activity at the pool level.

Table 19: Pool-Level Activity for Example 3

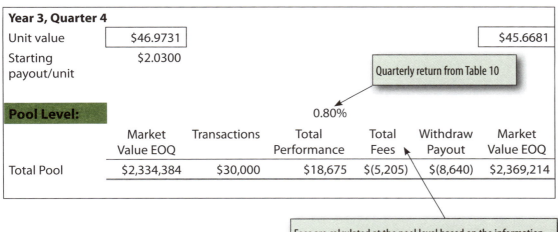

Year 3, Quarter 4						
Unit value	$46.9731					$45.6681
Starting payout/unit	$2.0300			*Quarterly return from Table 10*		
Pool Level:			0.80%			
	Market Value EOQ	Transactions	Total Performance	Total Fees	Withdraw Payout	Market Value EOQ
Total Pool	$2,334,384	$30,000	$18,675	$(5,205)	$(8,640)	$2,369,214

Fees are calculated at the pool level based on the information included in the "Endowment Funds Data" table 8.

Table 20 shows the activity for each fund, in both dollars and units, in two separate "buckets"—one to track principal transactions and a second to track income transactions.

Table 20: Fund-Level Activity for Example 3

Year 3, Quarter 4

Unit value	$46.9731	$45.6681
Starting payout/unit	$2.0300	

Fund Level:

Principal Dollars	Principal BOQ	Market Value BOQ	Transactions	Gain/Loss on Withdrawal	Principal EOQ	Market Value EOQ
Fund A	$285,000	$318,084	-	-	$285,000	$316,580
Fund B	$15,204	$15,883	-	-	$15,204	$15,807
Fund C	$222,000	$231,709	-	-	$222,000	$230,891
Fund D	$70,000	$87,401	$30,000	-	$100,000	$117,283
Fund E	$96,571	$101,693	-	-	$96,571	$101,210
Fund F	$35,000	$34,379	-	-	$35,000	$34,216
Fund G	$100,000	$97,946	-	-	$100,000	$97,601
Fund H	$1,500,000	$1,447,289	-	-	$1,500,000	$1,455,626
Total	$2,323,775	$2,334,384	$30,000	-	$2,353,775	$2,369,214

Affects the fund principal only.

Investment Return Dollars	Income BOQ	Interest/ Dividends and Realized Gains	Assess Fees	Payout per fund	Income EOQ
Fund A	$62,812	$11,769	$(795)	$(3,437)	$71,144
Fund B	$2,183	$588	$(40)	$(172)	$2,599
Fund C	$29,073	$8,573	$(290)	$(2,503)	$35,143
Fund D	$23,791	$3,234	-	-	$27,025
Fund E	$15,323	$3,763	$(254)	$(1,099)	$17,987
Fund F	$2,921	$1,272	$(86)	$(371)	$3,822
Fund G	$7,197	$3,624	$(122)	$(1,058)	$9,763
Fund H	$92,729	$53,550	$(3,618)	-	$146,279
Total	$236,029	$86,373	$(5,205)	$(8,640)	$313,762

3.70%

Calculated using the quarterly return information from the Table 10. For this quarter, interest/dividends = 1.09% and realized gains = 2.61% for total income of 3.70%.

Table 20: Fund-Level Activity for Example 3 (continued)

Principal Units	Principal Units BOQ	Units BOQ	Transactions	Principal Units EOQ	Total Units EOQ
EOQ"					
Fund A	5686.462	6,771.666	-	5,686.462	6,932.119
Fund B	304.089	338.133	-	304.089	346.137
Fund C	4415.639	4,932.803	-	4,415.639	5,055.852
Fund D	1392.887	1,860.658	638.663	2,031.550	2,568.169
Fund E	1927.345	2,164.911	-	1,927.345	2,216.217
Fund F	687.576	731.892	-	687.576	749.242
Fund G	1960.619	2,085.153	-	1,960.619	2,137.183
Fund H	29390.963	30,811.021	-	29,390.963	31,874.013
Total	45765.578	49,696.236	638.663	46,404.241	51,878.932

Income Units	Income Units BOQ	Interest / Dividends and Realized Gains	Assess Fees	Payout per fund	Income Units EOQ
Fund A	1,085.204	250.548	(16.925)	(73.170)	1,245.657
Fund B	34.044	12.518	(0.852)	(3.662)	42.049
Fund C	517.164	182.509	(6.174)	(53.286)	640.213
Fund D	467.771	68.848	-	-	536.619
Fund E	237.566	80.110	(5.407)	(23.396)	288.872
Fund F	44.316	27.079	(1.831)	(7.898)	61.666
Fund G	124.534	77.151	(2.597)	(22.524)	176.564
Fund H	1,420.058	1,140.014	(77.023)	-	2,483.049
Total	3,930.658	1,838.776	(110.808)	(183.935)	5,474.691

Table 21 shows the various calculations needed to track the average book value per unit, the test for underwater conditions, and the accumulated appreciation for each fund.

Table 21: Average Cost per Unit, Underwater Test, and Accumulated Appreciation Calculations for Example 3

Average Cost per Unit	End of Quarter
Fund A	$51.376
Fund B	51.433
Fund C	50.860
Fund D	49.461
Fund E	51.691
Fund F	51.815
Fund G	51.359
Fund H	51.650

> Calculated by dividing the EOQ fund principal and income balances by the total units at the end of the quarter.

Underwater Test True = not UW False = UW	EOQ Balances
Fund A	TRUE
Fund B	N/A
Fund C	TRUE
Fund D	TRUE
Fund E	N/A
Fund F	N/A
Fund G	FALSE
Fund H	FALSE

> Donor-restricted funds are tested to determine if they are underwater for purposes of determining the appropriate payout amount. If the market value is less than the Principal balance at the end of the quarter then the fund is deemed to be underwater.

Accumulated Appreciation	EOQ Accumulated Appreciation
Fund A	$31,580
Fund B	-
Fund C	$8,891
Fund D	$17,283
Fund E	-
Fund F	-
Fund G	$(2,399)
Fund H	$(44,374)
	$10,981

> For donor-restricted funds, the EOQ principal balance is subtracted from the EOQ market value to determine the accumulated appreciation.

Example 4—Unitized Method 3: Principal Only Approach, Transactions Based on End-of-Quarter Values

Example 4 illustrates a unitized method of managing the endowment pool and is similar to Example 2 (the Principal Only unitized method) except that unit values are calculated at the end of the quarter. The following assumptions are used in this example:

1. Only fund additions and fund withdrawals affect units. (Table 22 summarizes the effect on principal and transactions in units.)

Table 22: Effects on Principal or Investment Return and on Transaction in Units for Example 4

Transaction Description	Affects Principal or Investment Return	Transact in Units?
Gift received in an endowment fund / investment in a quasi-endowment fund	Principal	Yes
Allocation of investment pool return such as interest and dividends, realized gains and unrealized gains	Investment return	No
Application of spending policy and withdrawal of amounts available for spending	Investment return	No
Allocation of expenses or assessment of fees	Investment return	No
Reinvestment of unused amounts available for spending	Principal	Yes
Transfer from one fund to another within the pool	Principal	Yes
Withdrawal from a quasi-endowment	Principal	Yes
Divestment of an endowment fund from the pool to a separately held endowment	Principal	Yes

2. Fund investments and withdrawals are based on unit values at the end of the quarter. The market value per unit will be the same at the end of the quarter, both before and after money is added and withdrawn from each endowment.

3. The unit value is calculated quarterly.

4. Withdrawals are based on average cost.

5. The spending policy is calculated and based on the pool's market value per unit and applied to each fund based on the number of units held at the beginning of each quarter. At the fund level, the spending policy payout per unit is set, but the annual amount may vary, depending on the units held by the fund each quarter.

6. Note that Fund D is not receiving a payout while the fund accumulates. To accomplish this in a unitized model, a payout is calculated and then added back to the fund in both dollars and by purchasing units. This amount increases the fund's principal value. The accumulated undistributed investment returns are considered permanently restricted, as per the terms of the gift agreement.

7. Exceptions to fees at the fund level are "adjusted" by adding units to the fund to negate the impact of the fees on the unit value. The formula compares the allowed fee to the stated fee policy to determine the percentage required to negate the affect of the fee assessed at the pool level. For example, Fund C is assessed a fee of only 0.5%, even though the fee policy is 1.0%. Therefore, the allowed fee is one-half (50%) of the fee policy. The formula to adjust for this exception to the fee policy is [Fund C fee base] * [fee policy rate (1.0%)] * 50%. To avoid a "circular reference," this calculation is based on the unit value at the beginning of the quarter.

8. For funds underwater with fund parameters that prohibit a payout, the spending policy is not applied and no payout is calculated or withdrawn from the pool for that fund. Because the

withdrawal of the payout affects the unit value per share for all funds, those funds that did not receive a payout are assigned additional shares to counteract the effect of the payout withdrawal. The formula to add units is

    a–Calculate the payout per unit: X
    b–Multiply the payout per unit by the number of units in funds without payout: Y
    c–Calculate the dollar value of the payout on the funds that did not receive payout: X * Y = Z
    d–Divide the dollar value (Z) by the market value per unit (MVU) to get the number of units
       to add to the funds that did not receive a payout: Z ÷ MVU = units to add

9. For the donor-restricted endowments, the dollar value recorded as "principal" in the financial system is the historic dollar value and is classified as permanently restricted net assets. The difference between the market value of the fund (units * market value per unit) and the actual dollars recorded in the fund is temporarily restricted, until appropriated for spending.

Table 23 shows the activity at the pool level.

Table 23: Pool-Level Activity for Example 4

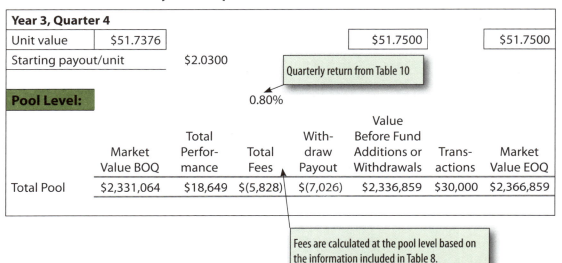

Year 3, Quarter 4							
Unit value	$51.7376				$51.7500		$51.7500
Starting payout/unit		$2.0300					
Pool Level:			0.80%				
					Value		
		Total		With-	Before Fund		
	Market	Perfor-	Total	draw	Additions or	Trans-	Market
	Value BOQ	mance	Fees	Payout	Withdrawals	actions	Value EOQ
Total Pool	$2,331,064	$18,649	$(5,828)	$(7,026)	$2,336,859	$30,000	$2,366,859

> Quarterly return from Table 10

> Fees are calculated at the pool level based on the information included in Table 8.

Table 24 shows the activity for each fund, in both dollars and units.

Table 24: Fund-Level Activity for Example 4

Year 3, Quarter 4

Unit value	$51.7376	$51.7500
Starting payout/unit	$2.0300	

Amounts used to calculate the number of units required to add back to the fund to adjust for the fees taken at the pool level. Amounts do not affect principal.

To reinvest income if directed by the donor. Increases the fund principal.

Affects fund principal only.

Fund Level: Dollars

	Fund Principal BOQ	Market Value BOQ	Fee Exception	Return Payout	Transactions	Gain/Loss on Withdrawal	Fund Principal EOQ	Market Value EOQ
Fund A	$285,000	$316,428	-	-	-	-	$285,000	$316,502
Fund B	$15,156	$15,683	-	-	-	-	$15,156	$15,687
Fund C	$222,000	$228,825	$3	-	-	-	$222,000	$228,882
Fund D	$77,813	$84,775	$2	$853	$30,000	-	$108,666	$115,650
Fund E	$101,576	$102,447	-	-	-	-	$101,576	$102,471
Fund F	$35,000	$34,631	-	-	-	-	$35,000	$34,639
Fund G	$100,000	$96,666	$1	-	-	-	$100,000	$96,691
Fund H	$1,500,000	$1,451,613	-	-	-	-	$1,500,000	$1,456,337
Total	$2,336,545	$2,331,068	$6	$853	$30,000	-	$2,367,398	$2,366,859

Fund Level: Units

	Total Units BOQ	Fee Exception	Return Payout	Units Before Fund Additions or Withdrawals	Unit Transactions	Total Units EOQ
Fund A	6,115.974	0.000	0.000	6,115.974	0.000	6,115.974
Fund B	303.122	0.000	0.000	303.122	0.000	303.122
Fund C	4,422.791	0.058	0.000	4,422.849	0.000	4,422.849
Fund D	1,638.554	0.039	16.487	1,655.080	579.710	2,234.790
Fund E	1,980.125	0.000	0.000	1,980.125	0.000	1,980.125
Fund F	669.358	0.000	0.000	669.358	0.000	669.358
Fund G	1,868.398	0.019	0.000	1,868.417	0.000	1,868.417
Fund H	28,057.214	0.000	84.566	28,141.780	0.000	28,141.780
Total	45,055.536	0.116	101.054	45,156.706	579.710	45,736.416

Table 25 shows the various calculations needed to track the average book value per unit, the test for underwater conditions, and the accumulated appreciation for each fund.

Table 25: Average Cost per Unit, Underwater Test, and Accumulated Appreciation Calculations for Example 4

Average Cost per Unit	End of Quarter
Fund A	46.599
Fund B	50.000
Fund C	50.194
Fund D	48.625
Fund E	51.298
Fund F	52.289
Fund G	53.521
Fund H	53.302

Calculated by dividing the EOQ fund principal balance by the total units at the end of the quarter.

Underwater Test True = not UW False = UW	EOQ Balances
Fund A	TRUE
Fund B	N/A
Fund C	TRUE
Fund D	TRUE
Fund E	N/A
Fund F	N/A
Fund G	FALSE
Fund H	FALSE

Donor-restricted funds are tested to determine if they are underwater for purposes of determining the appropriate payout amount. If the market value is less than the principal balance at the end of the quarter then the fund is deemed to be underwater.

Accumulated Appreciation	EOQ Accumulated Appreciation
Fund A	$31,502
Fund B	-
Fund C	$6,882
Fund D	$6,984
Fund E	-
Fund F	-
Fund G	$(3,309)
Fund H	$(43,663)
	$(1,604)

For donor-restricted funds, the EOQ principal balance is subtracted from the EOQ market value to determine the accumulated appreciation.

Summary of Examples

Table 26 provides a comparative summary of each of the examples.

Table 26: Comparison of Four Methods

Feature	Example 1	Example 2	Example 3	Example 4
Method	Dollarized	Unitized method 1	Unitized method 2	Unitized method 3
Period for unit value or allocations	Quarterly	Quarterly	Quarterly	Quarterly
Unit value for purchases or withdrawals	Not applicable	Unit value at the beginning of the period	Unit value at the beginning of the period	Unit value at the end of the period
Allocation base	Market value at the beginning of the period	Not applicable	Not applicable	Not applicable
Transactions that affect units	Not applicable	• Gift received in an endowment fund • Investment in a quasi-endowment fund • Transfer from one fund to another within the pool • Withdrawal from a quasi-endowment fund • Divestment of an endowment fund from the pool to a separately held endowment • Reinvestment of unused amounts available for spending	• Gift received in an endowment fund • Investment in a quasi-endowment fund • Transfer from one fund to another within the pool • Withdrawal from a quasi-endowment fund • Divestment of an endowment fund from the pool to a separately held endowment • Reinvestment of unused amounts available for spending • Interest and dividends • Realized gains/losses • Withdrawal of amounts available for spending • Allocation of expenses or assessment of fees	• Gift received in an endowment fund • Investment in a quasi-endowment fund • Transfer from one fund to another within the pool • Withdrawal from a quasi-endowment fund • Divestment of an endowment fund from the pool to a separately held endowment • Reinvestment of unused amounts available for spending

Feature	Example 1	Example 2	Example 3	Example 4
Transactions that affect unit market value	Not applicable	• Investment pool return such as interest and dividends, realized and unrealized gains/losses • Withdrawal of amounts available for spending • Allocation of expenses or assessment of fees	• Unrealized gains/losses	• Investment pool return such as interest and dividends, realized and unrealized gains/losses • Withdrawal of amounts available for spending • Allocation of expenses or assessment of fees
Method for calculating gain/loss on withdrawal of units	Not applicable	Average cost	Average cost	Average cost
Data for FASB disclosures detailing change in restriction classifications from the beginning of the year to the end of the year	• All amounts identifiable by each fund except the components of the investment return, which are derived from investment pool returns • Fees included in amounts appropriated for expenditure	• Beginning balance, ending balance, contributions, change in board-designated investments, and amounts appropriated for expenditure identifiable by fund • Investment returns calculated based on beginning and ending balances • Investment return components derived from investment pool returns • Fees included in investment return	• All amounts identifiable by each fund including interest/dividends by fund • Gains/losses on investments calculated based on all other components • Fees included in amounts appropriated for expenditure	• Beginning balance, ending balance, contributions, change in board-designated investments, and amounts appropriated for expenditure identifiable by fund • Investment returns calculated based on beginning and ending balances • Investment return components derived from investment pool returns • Fees included in investment return

Table 27 shows the market value by fund at the end of three years for each endowment tracking method and the proportion of the fund to the total pool for each method. It also shows the Year 3 payout for each fund in dollars and as a percentage of each fund's ending market value.

Table 27: Comparison of Outcomes of Four Methods

Example

Fund Balance After 3 years	1–Dollarized Method		2–Unitized Principal Only BOQ		3–Unitized Book Value BOQ		4–Unitized Principal Only EOQ	
	Dollars	Percent	Dollars	Percent	Dollars	Percent	Dollars	Percent
Fund								
A	$328,963	13.43%	$316,209	13.36%	$316,580	13.36%	$316,502	13.37%
B	15,552	0.63%	15,500	0.65%	15,807	0.67%	15,687	0.66%
C	236,474	9.64%	227,541	9.61%	230,891	9.75%	228,882	9.67%
D	117,535	4.79%	115,086	4.86%	117,283	4.95%	115,650	4.89%
E	109,017	4.44%	102,089	4.31%	101,210	4.27%	102,471	4.33%
F	35,746	1.46%	34,677	1.47%	34,216	1.44%	34,639	1.46%
G	101,999	4.16%	97,655	4.13%	97,601	4.12%	96,691	4.09%
H	1,507,468	61.45%	1,458,019	61.62%	1,455,626	61.44%	1,456,337	61.53%
TOTAL	$2,452,754	100.00%	$2,366,776	100.01%	$2,369,214	100.00%	$2,366,859	100.00%

Example

Payout in Year 3	1–Dollarized Method		2–Unitized Principal Only BOQ		3–Unitized Book Value BOQ		4–Unitized Principal Only EOQ	
	Dollars	Percent of Ending Market Value	Dollars	Percent of Ending Market Value	Dollars	Percent of Ending Market Value	Dollars	Percent of Ending Market Value
Fund								
A	$9,560	2.91%	$12,687	4.01%	$13,618	4.30%	$12,740	4.03%
B	780	5.02%	622	4.01%	680	4.30%	632	4.03%
C	6,936	2.93%	8,759	3.85%	9,518	4.12%	8,832	3.86%
D	-	0.00%	-	0.00%	-	0.00%	-	0.00%
E	3,500	3.21%	4,806	4.71%	5,110	5.05%	4,880	4.76%
F	1,448	4.05%	1,391	4.01%	1,472	4.30%	1,396	4.03%
G	1,880	1.84%	2,939	3.01%	4,185	4.29%	2,919	3.02%
H	25,152	1.67%	34,472	2.36%	36,750	2.52%	34,331	2.36%
TOTAL	$49,256		$65,676		$71,333		$65,730	

Sample Financial Statement Disclosures

Tables 28–31 show sample FASB disclosures in tabular format at the end of Year 3 for each method.

Table 28: Sample FASB Disclosure for Example 1

Example 1—Dollarized

Endowments by Net Asset Class At End of Year 3

	Unrestricted	Temporarily Restricted	Permanently Restricted	Total
Donor-restricted endowments	$-	$67,904	$2,224,535	$2,292,439
Board-designated endowments	160,315	-	-	160,315
Total funds	$160,315	$67,904	$2,224,535	$2,452,754

Funds A, C, D, G, H → Donor-restricted endowments

Funds B, E, F → Board-designated endowments

Change in Endowment Net Assets

	Unrestricted	Temporarily Restricted	Permanently Restricted	Total
Endowment net assets, end of Year 2	$201,208	$221,580	$1,678,260	$2,101,048
Investment:				
Investment income	5,405	4,328	58,347	68,079
Net depreciation (realized and unrealized)	(13,670)	(95,991)	(62,072)	(171,732)
Total investment return	(8,265)	(91,663)	(3,725)	(103,653)
Contributions	-	-	550,000	550,000
Appropriation of endowment assets for expenditure	(7,628)	(62,013)	-	(69,641)
Other changes:				
Reclassifications	-	-	-	-
Net change in board-designated endowment funds	(25,000)	-	-	(25,000)
Endowment net assets, end of Year 3	$160,315	$67,904	$2,224,535	$2,452,754

Breakdown of returns is calculated based on the interest/dividend returns for the period and the remainder is net depreciation. Compounded int/div for the year is 2.99%

Fees are included in the amount appropriated for expenditure.

Table 29: Sample FASB Disclosure for Example 2

Example 2—Unitized Method 1

Endowments by Net Asset Class At End of Year 3

	Unrestricted	Temporarily Restricted	Permanently Restricted	Total
Donor-restricted endowments	$(44,326)	$36,750	$2,222,086	$2,214,510
Board-designated endowments	152,266	-	-	160,315
Total funds	$107,940	$36,750	$2,222,086	$2,366,766

Change in Endowment Net Assets

	Unrestricted	Temporarily Restricted	Permanently Restricted	Total
Endowment net assets, end of Year 2	$190,719	$164,275	$1,675,861	$2,030,855
Investment:				
Investment income	4,465	3,005	58,274	65,745
Net depreciation (realized and unrealized)	(55,425)	(71,673)	(62,049)	(189,148)
Total investment return	(50,960)	(68,668)	(3,775)	(123,403)
Contributions	-	-	550,000	550,000
Appropriation of endowment assets for expenditure	(6,819)	(58,857)	-	(65,676)
Other changes:				
Reclassifications	-	-	-	-
Net change in board-designated endowment funds	(25,000)	-	-	(25,000)
Endowment net assets, end of Year 3	$107,940	$36,750	$2,222,086	$2,366,776

Funds A, C, D, G, H

Funds B, E, F

Breakdown of returns is calculated based on the interest/dividend returns for the period and the remainder is net depreciation. Compounded int/div for the year is 2.99%

Calculated value for purposes of the disclosure, not derived from actual transactions for each fund.

Table 30: Sample FASB Disclosure for Example 3

Example 3—Unitized Method 2

Endowments by Net Asset Class At End of Year 3

	Unrestricted	Temporarily Restricted	Permanently Restricted	Total
Donor-restricted endowments	$(46,773)	$40,471	$2,224,283	$2,217,981
Board-designated endowments	151,233	-	-	151,233
Total funds	$104,460	$40,471	$2,224,283	$2,369,214

Funds A, C, D, G, H → Donor-restricted endowments

Funds B, E, F → Board-designated endowments

Change in Endowment Net Assets

	Unrestricted	Temporarily Restricted	Permanently Restricted	Total
Endowment net assets, end of Year 2	$189,797	$167,873	$1,678,051	$2,035,721
Investment:				
Investment income	3,675	64,255	4,104	72,034
Net depreciation (realized and unrealized)	(54,956)	(109,711)	(7,872)	(172,539)
Total investment return	(51,281)	(45,456)	(3,768)	(100,505)
Contributions	-	-	550,000	550,000
Appropriation of endowment assets for expenditure	(9,056)	(81,946)	-	(91,002)
Other changes:				
Reclassifications	-	-	-	-
Net change in board-designated endowment funds	(25,000)	-	-	(25,000)
Endowment net assets, end of Year 3	$104,460	$40,471	$2,224,283	$2,369,214

Returns are not prorated. Amounts come directly from allocations to each fund. → Endowment net assets, end of Year 2

Fees are included in the amount appropriated for expenditure → Appropriation of endowment assets for expenditure

Table 31: Sample FASB Disclosure for Example 4

Example 4—Unitized Method 4

Endowments by Net Asset Class At End of Year 3

	Unrestricted	Temporarily Restricted	Permanently Restricted	Total
Donor-restricted endowments	$(46,972)	$38,384	$2,222,650	$2,214,062
Board-designated endowments	152,797	-	-	152,797
Total funds	$105,825	$38,384	$2,222,650	$2,366,859

Change in Endowment Net Assets

	Unrestricted	Temporarily Restricted	Permanently Restricted	Total
Endowment net assets, end of Year 2	$193,719	$159,554	$1,676,842	$2,030,115
Investment:				
Investment income	4,478	2,959	58,297	65,735
Net depreciation (realized and unrealized)	(60,464)	(65,307)	(62,489)	(188,261)
Total investment return	(55,986)	(62,348)	(4,192)	(122,526)
Contributions	-	-	550,000	550,000
Appropriation of endowment assets for expenditure	(6,908)	(58,822)	-	(65,730)
Other changes:				
Reclassifications	-	-	-	-
Net change in board-designated endowment funds	(25,000)	-	-	(25,000)
Endowment net assets, end of Year 3	$105,825	$38,384	$2,222,650	$2,366,859

Funds A, C, D, G, H

Funds B, E, F

Breakdown of returns is calculated based on the interest/dividend returns for the period and the remainder is net depreciation. Compounded int/div for the year is 2.99%.

Calculated value for purposes of the disclosure, not derived from actual transactions for each fund.

APPENDIX

Appendix A—Glossary of Terms

Appropriation	Making financial resources available for expenditure.
Board-designated fund	A type of quasi-endowment established by action of a governing body (or its delegate) to invest a portion of currently available resources for the long term rather than using it for current purposes. [12]
Book value	The amount of an investment or investment portfolio comprised of the purchases, sales, and accumulated realized gains or losses resulting from sales of the investments. The book value does not include increases or decreases in the market prices of investments prior to those investments being sold.
Corpus	Another term for "principal."
Fund	An identifier used to indicate financial resources set aside for a specific purpose. Endowments and similar funds are comprised of an initial deposit, subsequent deposits (if any), and accumulated investment returns added to the investment and/or available for future use.
Funds functioning as endowment	Resources set aside that operate similarly to an endowment fund. A principal amount is invested, generally for a minimum term set by the institution, and the investment returns on the principal are available for expenditure. After the minimum term, both the principal and interest are available for use.
Historic dollar value	A concept introduced by the Uniform Management of Institutional Funds Act (UMIFA) for donor-initiated endowment funds. The historic dollar value of an endowment fund is comprised of donor gift(s) to the endowment, as well as investment returns directed by the donor to be reinvested in the endowment and not available for expenditure.
Investment pool	Assets of many endowments and similar funds commingled into one investment portfolio.
Investment returns	The resources earned on stocks, bonds, or other ownership or creditor interests, comprised of interest income and dividends, gains or losses on sales of holdings, and changes in the market values of holdings not yet sold.
Principal	The portion of an endowment or similar fund that represents the amount invested and generally not available for appropriation. In certain situations the principal may be used to meet short-term spending needs, with the intention of replacing the principal amount withdrawn with future investment returns.
Quasi-endowment	See "Funds functioning as endowment."
Spending formula	The means by which an organization determines the amount of investment returns available for current use. Generally, spending formulas are designed to meet the organization's need for current income while at the same time protecting the purchasing power of the resources for future generations.

[12] NACUBO Financial and Accounting Reporting Manual 352.35

Appendix B—Cross Walk: FASB Standards Superseded by FASB Codification

SFAS	FASB Codification
SFAS 116, *Accounting for Contributions Received and Contributions Made*	ASC 958-605
SFAS 117, *Financial Statements of Not-for-Profit Organizations*	ASC 958-205
FASB Staff Position (FSP), Financial Accounting Standard (FAS) 117-1, *Endowments of Not-for-Profit Organizations: Net Asset Classification of Funds Subject to an Enacted Version of the Uniform Management of Institutional Funds Act, and Enhanced Disclosures for All Endowment Funds*	ASC 958-205
SFAS 124, *Accounting for Certain Investments Held by Not-for-Profit Organizations*	ASC 958-320

Appendix C—Resources for Additional Information

University Sample Data (referenced on page 21 and page 29) to help you build your own unitization model
http://www.nacubo.org/Documents/Products/NC3117_University_Sample_Data.xls

NACUBO College and University Business Administration, Fifth Edition
Chapter 9, "Endowment Management"

NACUBO *Financial and Accounting Reporting Manual (FARM)*

For institutions with a FARM subscription:

- www.nacubo.org
- Go to "My NACUBO"
- Go to "Online Subscriptions"

To subscribe to FARM:
- www.nacubo.org
- Go to Products/Financial Accounting and Reporting Manual - FARM

IRS Form 990, Report of Organization Exempt from Income Tax
http://www.irs.gov/charities/article/0,,id=218927,00.html

The Uniform Law Commission (ULC) and UPMIFA
http://uniformlaws.org/ActSummary.aspx?title=Prudent Management of Institutional Funds Act